MW00488451

THIS JOURNAL BELONGS TO:

....

DATE:

....

· · · · · · INTRODUCTION · · · · · ·

*I*n the summer of 2014, my love of Scripture met my love of handwriting when I began the hobby of hand lettering some of my favorite Bible verses. I picked out a pretty journal and filled the pages with wonderful truths from God's Word, and I gave that journal to my oldest daughter. As I continued with the hobby of hand lettering Scripture, I soon realized that what I was actually doing was meditating on the Word of God, carefully considering every letter and every word I drew from the Bible. I hope that similarly, the illustrated Bible verses in this journal will encourage you to take time to pause and consider the timeless truth God has preserved for us through the ages in His Word.

The Bible is filled with so many wonderful and encouraging words for the Christian, powered by the Holy Spirit to spur us on to faith and good works. Only when we are in Christ may we lay claim to God's promises.

This journal contains just a tiny portion of the greatest book ever written and the greatest story ever told. May it leave you thirsting for more. Open your Bible, and may the Holy Spirit draw you evermore to Christ, who alone can satisfy.

—Debbie

For from him and through him and to him are all things.
To him be the glory forever! Amen.

ROMANS 11:36 ESV

For My yoke is easy and My burden is light.

MATTHEW 11:30 ❀ NKJV

Come to Me, all you who labor and are heavy laden, and I will give you rest.

MATTHEW 11:28 NKJV

Take My yoke upon you and learn from Me, for I am gentle
and lowly in heart, and you will find rest for your souls.

MATTHEW 11:29 NKJV

For I am not ashamed of the gospel of Christ, for it is the power
of God to salvation for everyone who believes.

ROMANS 1:16 NKJV

So faith comes from hearing, and hearing through the word of Christ.

ROMANS 10:17 ESV

BY THE word of the LORD THE HEAVENS WERE MADE.

PSALM 33:6 ✿ NIV

In the beginning was the Word, and the Word was with God,
and the Word was God.

JOHN 1:1 NIV

Then God said, "Let there be light," and there was light. God saw
that the light was good, and God separated the light from the darkness.

GENESIS 1:3–4 HCSB

God created man in His own image, in the image of God
He created him; male and female He created them.

GENESIS 1:27 NASB

The heavens declare the glory of God;
the skies proclaim the work of his hands.

PSALM 19:1 NIV

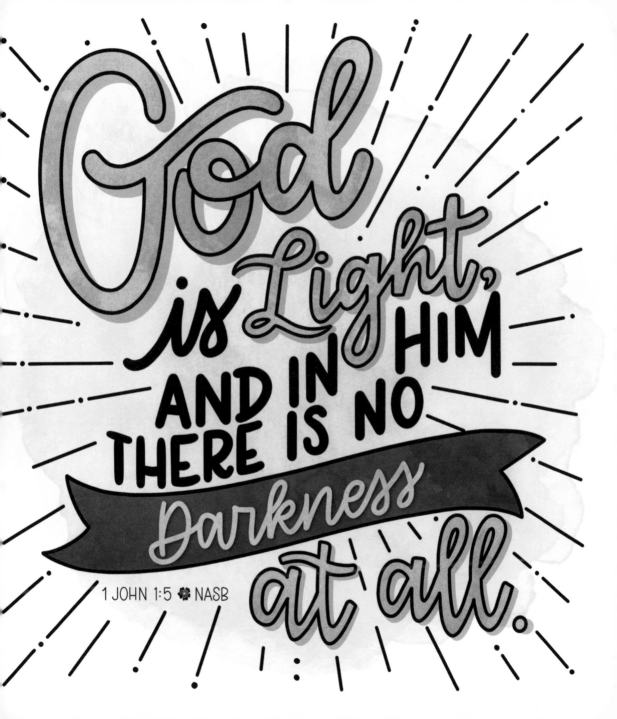

If we walk in the light, as he is in the light, we have fellowship with one another, and the blood of Jesus his Son cleanses us from all sin.

1 JOHN 1:7 ESV

Blessed are those who hunger and thirst for righteousness,
for they shall be filled.

MATTHEW 5:6 NKJV

Seek first the kingdom of God and His righteousness,
and all these things shall be added to you.

MATTHEW 6:33 NKJV

Let us then with confidence draw near to the throne of grace,
that we may receive mercy and find grace to help in time of need.

HEBREWS 4:16 ESV

THE LORD IS righteous HIS IN ALL WAYS AND gracious IN ALL HIS ACTS.

PSALM 145:17 ❀ HCSB

For God so loved the world that He gave His only begotten Son,
that whoever believes in Him should not perish but have everlasting life.

JOHN 3:16 NKJV

If you confess with your mouth that Jesus is Lord and believe in your heart that God raised him from the dead, you will be saved.

ROMANS 10:9 ESV

For with the heart one believes and is justified,
and with the mouth one confesses and is saved.

ROMANS 10:10 ESV

Jesus told him, "I am the way, the truth, and the life.
No one comes to the Father except through Me."

JOHN 14:6 HCSB

FOR THERE IS
NO OTHER NAME UNDER
heaven
MEN
GIVEN BY
AMONG WHICH
we must be
SAVED.

ACTS 4:12 ❀ ESV

He was pierced for our transgressions, he was crushed
for our iniquities; the punishment that brought us peace was
on him, and by his wounds we are healed.

ISAIAH 53:5 NIV

Blessed are your eyes because they see, and your ears because they hear.

MATTHEW 13:16 NIV

His name shall be called Wonderful Counselor,
Mighty God, Everlasting Father, Prince of Peace.

ISAIAH 9:6 ESV

This hope will not disappoint us, because God's love has been poured out
in our hearts through the Holy Spirit who was given to us.

ROMANS 5:5 HCSB

"And surely I am with you always, to the very end of the age."

MATTHEW 28:20 ❀ NIV

> And if I go and prepare a place for you, I will come back and take you
> to be with me that you also may be where I am.
>
> JOHN 14:3 NIV

The Word became flesh and dwelt among us. We observed his glory,
the glory as the one and only Son from the Father, full of grace and truth.

JOHN 1:14 CSB

Having been justified by faith, we have peace with God
through our Lord Jesus Christ.

ROMANS 5:1 NKJV

Now faith is the assurance of things hoped for,
the conviction of things not seen.

HEBREWS 11:1 ESV

THEY THAT WAIT
UPON LORD
THE

SHALL RENEW
THEIR
strength;
THEY SHALL
mount up
WITH WINGS
AS EAGLES.

ISAIAH 40:31 ❀ KJV

Give thanks to the LORD, for he is good;
his faithful love endures forever.

PSALM 107:1 CSB

For he satisfies the longing soul,
and the hungry soul he fills with good things.

PSALM 107:9 ESV

Let the morning bring me word of your unfailing love,
for I have put my trust in you.

PSALM 143:8 NIV

I remain confident of this: I will see the goodness
of the LORD in the land of the living.

PSALM 27:13 NIV

BEHOLD,
GOD
IS MY
Salvation;
I WILL
trust AND NOT BE
AFRAID.

ISAIAH 12:2 ❀ NKJV

The Lord God is my strength and my song,
and he has become my salvation.

ISAIAH 12:2 ESV

The fear of the LORD is the beginning of wisdom,
and the knowledge of the Holy One is understanding.

PROVERBS 9:10 NASB

I have hidden your word in my heart
that I might not sin against you.

PSALM 119:11 NIV

You will keep in perfect peace those whose minds are steadfast,
because they trust in you.

ISAIAH 26:3 NIV

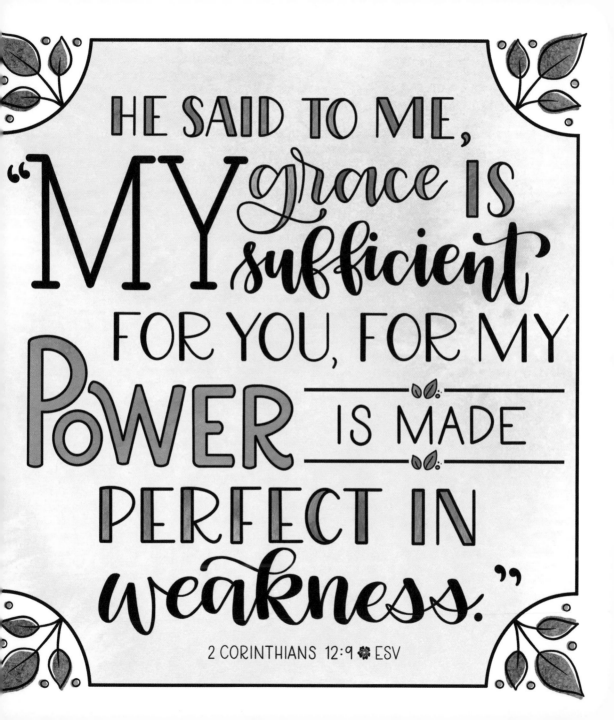

HE SAID TO ME, "MY *grace* IS *sufficient* FOR YOU, FOR MY POWER IS MADE PERFECT IN *weakness.*"

2 CORINTHIANS 12:9 ❀ ESV

Therefore I will boast all the more gladly of my weaknesses,
so that the power of Christ may rest upon me.

2 CORINTHIANS 12:9 ESV

The steadfast love of the LORD never ceases; his mercies never come to an end;
they are new every morning; great is your faithfulness.

LAMENTATIONS 3:22–23 ESV

Trust in the LORD with all your heart and do not lean on your own understanding. In all your ways acknowledge Him, and He will make your paths straight.

PROVERBS 3:5–6 NASB

The name of the LORD is a strong tower;
the righteous run to it and are safe.

PROVERBS 18:10 NKJV

Thy word is a

LAMP

unto my

FEET,

and a

LIGHT

unto my path.

PSALM 119:105 ❀ KJV

The grass withers, the flower fades,
but the word of our God stands forever.

ISAIAH 40:8 NKJV

Be anxious for nothing, but in everything by prayer and supplication,
with thanksgiving, let your requests be made known to God.

PHILIPPIANS 4:6 NKJV

And the peace of God, which surpasses all understanding,
will guard your hearts and minds through Christ Jesus.

PHILIPPIANS 4:7 NKJV

Whatever is true, whatever is noble, whatever is right, whatever is pure, whatever is lovely, whatever is admirable—if anything is excellent or praiseworthy—think about such things.

PHILIPPIANS 4:8 NIV

WHAT DOES THE
LORD
REQUIRE OF YOU BUT TO
DO JUSTLY, TO LOVE MERCY,
AND TO WALK HUMBLY
WITH YOUR
God?
MICAH 6:8 ❀ NKJV

Be kind to one another, tender-hearted, forgiving each other,
just as God in Christ also has forgiven you.

EPHESIANS 4:32 NASB

You were once darkness, but now you are light in the Lord.
Walk as children of light.

EPHESIANS 5:8 NKJV

I am sure of this, that he who began a good work in you
will bring it to completion at the day of Jesus Christ.

PHILIPPIANS 1:6 ESV

By grace you have been saved through faith. And this is not your own doing;
it is the gift of God, not a result of works, so that no one may boast.

EPHESIANS 2:8–9 ESV

THE FRUIT OF THE SPIRIT IS

LOVE, JOY, PEACE, patience, KINDNESS, goodness, faithfulness, GENTLENESS, self-control.

GALATIANS 5:22-23 ❧ NASB

If anyone is in Christ, he is a new creation.
The old has passed away; behold, the new has come.

2 CORINTHIANS 5:17 ESV

For we are his workmanship, created in Christ Jesus for good works,
which God prepared beforehand, that we should walk in them.

EPHESIANS 2:10 ESV

One thing I have desired of the LORD, that will I seek:
that I may dwell in the house of the LORD all the days of my life.

PSALM 27:4 NKJV

If God is for us, who can be against us?

ROMANS 8:31 NKJV

The life I now live in the flesh I live by faith in the Son of God,
who loved me and gave himself for me.

GALATIANS 2:20 ESV

May the God of hope fill you with all joy and peace as you believe so that
you may overflow with hope by the power of the Holy Spirit.

ROMANS 15:13 CSB

Grow in the grace and knowledge of our Lord and Savior Jesus Christ.
To Him be the glory both now and to the day of eternity.

2 PETER 3:18 HCSB

The Lord grants favor and honor;
he does not withhold the good from those who live with integrity.

PSALM 84:11 CSB

I have loved you with an everlasting love;
I have drawn you with unfailing kindness.

JEREMIAH 31:3 NIV

Guide me in your truth and teach me, for you are God my Savior,
and my hope is in you all day long.

PSALM 25:5 NIV

Create in me a clean heart, O God; and renew a right spirit within me.

PSALM 51:10 KJV

I will rejoice in the LORD,
I will be joyful in God my Savior.

HABAKKUK 3:18 NIV

Rejoice ALWAYS; PRAY without CEASING; IN EVERYTHING give THANKS.

1 THESSALONIANS 5:16-18 ❧ NASB

If I rise on the wings of the dawn, if I settle on the far side of the sea, even there your hand will guide me, your right hand will hold me fast.

PSALM 139:9–10 NIV

Behold what manner of love the Father has bestowed on us,
that we should be called children of God!

1 JOHN 3:1 NKJV

He who dwells in the secret place of the Most High
shall abide under the shadow of the Almighty.

PSALM 91:1 NKJV

I can do all things through Christ who strengthens me.

PHILIPPIANS 4:13 NKJV

WE KNOW THAT
God CAUSES all things
TO WORK together FOR good
TO THOSE who love GOD.

ROMANS 8:28 ❧ NASB

I will strengthen you, I will help you,
I will uphold you with my righteous right hand.

ISAIAH 41:10 ESV

For as high as the heavens are above the earth,
so great is his love for those who fear him.

PSALM 103:11 NIV

For the LORD is good; His mercy is everlasting,
and His truth endures to all generations.

PSALM 100:5 NKJV

Copyright © 2021 by Debbie Bratton

Cover art: Debbie Bratton. Cover copyright © 2021 by Hachette Book Group, Inc.

Hachette Book Group supports the right to free expression and the value of copyright. The purpose of copyright is to encourage writers and artists to produce the creative works that enrich our culture.

The scanning, uploading, and distribution of this book without permission is a theft of the author's intellectual property. If you would like permission to use material from the book (other than for review purposes), please contact permissions@hbgusa.com. Thank you for your support of the author's rights.

Ellie Claire
Hachette Book Group
1290 Avenue of the Americas, New York, NY 10104
ellieclaire.com

First Edition: March 2021

Ellie Claire is a division of Hachette Book Group, Inc. The Ellie Claire name and logo are trademarks of Hachette Book Group, Inc.

The publisher is not responsible for websites (or their content) that are not owned by the publisher.

Bible quotations are taken from the New King James Version® (KJV). Copyright © 1982 by Thomas Nelson. Used by permission. All rights reserved. | The Holy Bible, New International Version®(NIV)®. Copyright © 1973, 1978, 1984, 2011 by Biblica. Used by permission of Zondervan. All rights reserved worldwide. | THE NEW AMERICAN STANDARD BIBLE® (NASB), Copyright © 1960, 1962, 1963, 1968, 1971, 1972, 1973, 1975, 1977, 1995 by The Lockman Foundation. Used by permission. | The Holy Bible, English Standard Version® (ESV®), copyright © 2001 by Crossway Bibles, a publishing ministry of Good News Publishers. | The Christian Standard Bible (CSB) Copyright © 2017 by Holman Bible Publishers. Used by permission. Christian Standard Bible®, and CSB® are federally registered trademarks of Holman Bible Publishers, all rights reserved. | The Holman Christian Standard Bible®, Copyright © 1999, 2000, 2002, 2003, 2009 by Holman Bible Publishers. Used by permission. Holman Christian Standard Bible® (HCSB), Holman CSB®, and HCSB® are federally registered trademarks of Holman Bible Publishers. | New American Standard Bible® (NASB), copyright © 1960, 1962, 1963, 1968, 1972, 1975, 1977, 1995 by The Lockman Foundation. Used by permission.

Print book interior art by Debbie Bratton; colorization by Jeff Jansen | Aestheticsoup.net.
Interior design by Melissa Reagan

ISBN: 978-1-5460-1489-8

Printed in China
APS
10 9 8 7 6 5 4 3 2 1